LAND OF THE FREE

The Bald Eagle

Anne Hempstead

Heinemann Library
Chicago, Illinois

© 2006 Heinemann
Published by Heinemann Library
A division of Reed Elsevier Inc.
Chicago, IL
Customer Service 888-363-4266
Visit our website at www.heinemannraintree.com

For more information address the publisher:
Raintree, 100 N. LaSalle, Suite 1200, Chicago IL 60602

Printed in China by WKT Company Limited

10 09 08 07 06
10 9 8 7 6 5 4 3 2 1

ISBN 1-4034-7003-0 (hc) -- ISBN 1-4034-7010-3 (pb)
Library of Congress Cataloging-in-Publication Data:

Cataloging-in-publication data is on file at the Library of Congress.

Photo research: Julie Laffin

Acknowledgments
The author and publisher are grateful to the following for permission to reproduce copyright material:
p.4 © Getty Images/PhotoDisc, pp.6, 12, 13, 19, 27 © Corbis/Bettmann, p.9 U.S. Mint, p.10 © The Bridgeman Art Library/ Private Collection, p.14 © Getty Images/Hulton Archive, pp.16, 20 Library of Congress, p.18 The Granger Collection, p.22 Oklahoma Museum of History, p. 24 © Corbis/K.J. Historical.

Cover: © Getty Images/PhotoDisc

The paper used to print this book comes from sustainable resources.

Contents

Chapter One:
A Spirited Symbol

As it soars through the sky, the eagle seems to be the essence of freedom and courage. Since ancient times, the eagle's broad wings, strong talons, and fierce expression have captured people's imaginations. In Greek mythology, the eagle was the only bird that lived among the gods on Mount Olympus. Some Native Americans believed that the bird caused thunder as it flew. Others considered the eagle to be a messenger from the creator of the universe. In 1782 the founders of the United States chose the bald eagle as the national **symbol** of the United States. Since then it has been one of the most treasured **emblems** of American democracy.

A great, noble bird

The bald eagle's noble looks and behavior led to its selection as a national symbol. The eagle has a stately appearance with its pure white head and tail; a yellow beak, eyes, and feet; and brown feathers on its body. An adult male bald eagle can grow to be three feet (one meter) long, and the female is several inches larger.

The eagle's wingspan is between six and eight feet (about two meters)—as wide as a basketball player is tall. Despite their size, bald eagles are not very heavy. They only weigh five to thirteen pounds (two to six kilograms)—about as much as a large housecat. Despite its name, the bald eagle is not really bald at all. The adult bird's white head feathers are the reason for its name. The word *bald* means "white" as well as "hairless."

Nations and symbols

Symbols can be used to represent a country's beliefs and ideals. When a symbol or **emblem** connected with a particular country appears on flags, buildings, money, and documents, it signals that the object is from that country.

Some early symbols were images carved from wood, metal, or stone. These images were placed at the top of poles and carried to show that the holder belonged to a certain tribe or was loyal to a specific leader. The image of the eagle became a symbol of power in the Roman Empire. Roman armies marched with long staffs topped with eagles.

. 2. Rußland.

The crest of the Romanovs, the imperial family of Russia, features eagles, as do the crests of many other royal families.

Common Symbols

A symbol is something that stands for something else. Symbols are useful because they get their ideas across quickly. Here are some symbols you might recognize.

Judaism

love

Christianity

Islam

peace

In the 1100s, **coats of arms** and **heraldry** (the making of coats of arms) came into use. Scholars think coats of arms were invented by European nobility. The first known coat of arms was a design painted on a knight's shield. It showed objects that related to the knight's family history. When fighting in tournaments and battles, knights wore their family's coat of arms on their shields and armor. This allowed the knight to be easily recognized by friends and enemies. A king or duke's coat of arms could not be used by any other family.

Coats of arms developed into a complicated visual language. Objects, shapes, lines, colors, and the position of the items on the background all took on special meanings. The traditional meaning of an eagle in heraldry is "nobility," "strength," and "bravery." If the eagle's wings are spread this means "protection."

The United States was not the first country to choose a specific type of eagle as a national symbol. A black eagle has been a symbol for Germany since about 1200. In the 1300s, Poland was ruled by a king with a white eagle in his family crest and it has been the country's symbol ever since. Russia's emblem, a two-headed golden eagle, has been in use, off and on, since at least the 1400s.

America's patriotic symbols

The United States was founded on the idea of "liberty and justice for all." Most American **patriotic symbols** have this idea as their primary meaning. Other popular American symbols include the U.S. flag, the Liberty Bell, and the Statue of Liberty.

Over time the bald eagle has come to stand for the U.S. government itself. When people see pictures of the bald eagle on money or stamps, they can tell right away what country those items come from.

National symbols like the bald eagle give people an easy way to show their patriotism, or love for their country. When people fly a flag in their yard or choose a mailbox with a bald eagle on it, other people can tell that the person feels patriotic. During wartime many people choose to display pictures of bald eagles looking angry. These pictures show the person feels the country is ready to fight. Other people may choose pictures of a bald eagle looking sad, or crying. These pictures show that the person feels sad about what the country is currently going through. When George Washington became president in 1789, he wore a brown suit with eagle buttons to show his patriotism.

The eagle on coins

The eagle has appeared on many types of U.S. currency, or national money. For many years, the eagle appeared on gold coins worth twenty, ten, five, and two and a half dollars. The ten-dollar coin was called an "eagle," so the five-dollar coin became a "half eagle" (because it was worth half as much), and the $2.50 coin was a "quarter eagle." Those coins began appearing in 1795 and 1796. A twenty-dollar coin—the "double eagle"—appeared in 1850.

In 1933 double eagles were discontinued and supposedly destroyed. Amazingly, though, an employee at the U.S. Mint stole ten of them. Nine were eventually found and destroyed—that last double eagle became the most valuable coin on earth. It was auctioned in 2002 and sold for $6.6 million.

Chapter Two:
A Symbol for a New Nation

After winning independence from England, Americans were faced with the task of building a new nation. The **Constitution** united the former **colonies** under one national, or **federal**, government. But the leaders knew that, if the country was to be a success, its people needed to think and feel like citizens of the United States. It was also important that the United States be recognized as a country of equal status with the other countries of the world.

To help create a national identity, **Congress** decided that a capital city should be built as a home for the new government. The city would represent the ideals of the Constitution. Its buildings would be beautiful and grand like the temples in Ancient Greece and Rome. The streets would be wide and lined with monuments to the heroes of the Revolutionary War. There would be plenty of open spaces where everyday people could mingle with government officials. The city would be recognized by the world as the capital of democracy.

Old symbols, new meanings

Congress wanted two national **emblems**: a flag and a **coat of arms** or "Great Seal." These had practical purposes. The flag was needed for American ships, so that they could be easily recognized at sea. An official seal was necessary for the signing of **treaties** and other documents. But the leaders also believed that a national flag and coat of arms would help people feel pride and unity in the new nation. The flag and Great Seal would stand for not only the U.S. government, but for its people as well.

Americans were used to expressing political ideas through **symbols**. In 1754, before the **colonies** had achieved independence, Benjamin Franklin published what many consider America's first political cartoon. It showed a rattlesnake cut into pieces with the caption "Join, or Die." The rattlesnake became a popular symbol of colonial unity against the British. Rebellious groups created flags using a picture of the snake, often accompanied by the warning "Don't tread on me."

Before the Revolutionary War, the rattlesnake became a popular symbol of colonial unity. This flag is similar to the first U.S. Navy flag.

Patriots adopted other symbols to show their desire to be free of British rule. The Liberty Bell, with its inscription "Proclaim Liberty throughout all the land," was one of the most stirring symbols for patriots during the Revolutionary War. Another popular emblem was the "Liberty Cap," a knitted hat with a tassel. The hat was inspired by a legend of a Roman slave who was said to have worn such a cap when he was set free. Patriots wore little "Liberty Cap" pins to show their dislike of being ruled by the king of England. The image of the cap also was forged into weathervanes or carved from wood and carried on the end of a pole. The cap later was used as a symbol of freedom in the French Revolution.

The liberty cap was not the only Roman symbol that interested Americans. The framers of the Constitution had written the **Constitution** based on Greek and Roman political thought. Now they turned to those ancient **civilizations** for more inspiration. One of the reasons the eagle was chosen for the Great Seal of the United States was Rome's use of an eagle as its symbol.

The Roman Goddess of Liberty was a popular Roman symbol adopted by early Americans.

Designing the Great Seal

Benjamin Franklin, Thomas Jefferson, and John Adams joined together to design a **coat of arms** and "Great Seal." After a lot of discussion and disagreement, they came to an agreement and submitted an idea to **Congress**. The idea was rejected. The lawmakers asked two other committees to work on the seal. William Barton, a lawyer and **heraldry** scholar, added a small white eagle to the front of the seal.

Six years after the first design was proposed, the matter was turned over to the Secretary of Congress, Charles Thomson. Thomson combined elements from all the previous designs into a final version. He changed Barton's small white eagle to a large bald eagle, a bird that is native to the United States. Thomson wanted a bird that would be a **symbol** of independence from Europe. He thought using a bird that could be found in Europe would send the wrong message. On July 20, 1782, the design was finally approved.

Charles Thomas designed the Great Seal.

~ 14 ~

The patriotic turkey?

Benjamin Franklin did not like the choice of the bald eagle as the national bird. "For my own part, I wish the bald eagle had not been chosen as the representative of our country; he is a bird of bad moral character," he wrote in a letter to his daughter. Franklin preferred another American native— the wild turkey. He wrote: *"The turkey is in comparison a much more respectable bird..a true original native of America... He is besides, (though a little vain and silly, it is true, but not the worse* **emblem** *for that,) a bird of courage, and would not hesitate to attack a [soldier] of the British guards, who should presume to invade his farmyard with a red coat on."*

It is often said that Franklin proposed the wild turkey as an alternative to the bald eagle as national bird, but this probably never happened. The letter in which Franklin talked about his admiration for the turkey was written in 1784, two years after Congress had already settled on the bald eagle as the national bird.

Franklin's dislike of the eagle was based on its behavior. In the wild, eagles save all of their energy for hunting. A bird will sit still, resting and watching, for hours. Bald eagles have also been known to spy on other birds while they catch fish. Once the fish is caught, the eagle steals the fish away. Franklin thought the bald eagle was lazy and dishonest.

Front of Great Seal

1. Bald eagle 2. The Latin on this scroll means "Out of many, one," referring to the idea that the United States was created from thirteen separate colonies. 3. The olive branches symbolize the power of peace. 4. The arrows symbolize the power of war. 5. The blue on the shield represents the power of the president and Congress; the red and white stripes represent the individual states supporting the president. 6. The thirteen stars represent the thirteen colonies; together they are forming a new star, representing the new nation.

Back of Great Seal

1. The pyramid stands for strength and duration. 2. The eye and the motto Annuit Coeptis together mean that God oversees and approves of the American cause 3. 1776 in Roman Numerals 4. This Latin phrase means "A new order of the ages."

Chapter Three:
The Great Seal at Work

When the Great Seal appears on an object, it means that the object is officially from the U.S. government. It is used to seal important documents such as **treaties** and **proclamations** about 2,000 to 3,000 times a year. It also appears on coins, stamps, stationery, publications, flags, military uniforms, and passports—anything the government owns or uses. The seal is also over the door of every U.S. government building around the world. The Great Seal cannot appear on souvenirs or other unofficial objects.

In 1789 **Congress** created the State Department and gave it the job of keeping the seal safe. Secretary of Congress Charles Thomson carried the seal by hand to President Washington, who gave it to Thomas Jefferson, the Secretary of State. Today the seal is no longer portable. It is kept in a glass enclosure in the Exhibit Hall of the State Department in Washington, D.C. The enclosure is kept locked at all times—even during the sealing of a document. When a treaty is ready for sealing, an officer of the State Department carries the paper into the glass enclosure. Once inside, the officer presses the seal onto the document, creating an imprint.

A symbol of government

The bald eagle was quickly accepted as the **symbol** of the U.S. government. People liked its powerful and dignified image. The eagle was incorporated into designs for the three branches of government. Many carvings and paintings of eagles are found in the U.S. Capitol building. The most famous is the Eagle and Shield in the Old Senate Chamber. This life-sized wooden eagle, perched on the canopy over the vice president's chair, looks like it is about to fly across the room.

A silver eagle sits proudly on top of the mace of the House of Representatives. The mace is a staff, or long club, that symbolizes the authority of the Sergeant at Arms to

The U.S. Eagle presides over the Old Senate Chamber in the U.S. Capitol.

maintain order in the House. Like the **coat of arms**, the mace was used in the Middle Ages. Originally, it was a weapon used in battle. These days the leader of the House uses the mace to signal that a certain number of congress people must be present to vote on a law. Sometimes it is placed in front of a member whose behavior is considered out of order.

The Supreme Court uses a seal that looks similar to the Great Seal. However, the Court's seal has a single star under the eagle's claws. This star symbolizes the "one Supreme Court" created by the **Constitution**.

In 1880 President Rutherford B. Hayes had the presidential seal created. The design of the seal is similar to that of the Great Seal. At first, the eagle on the presidential seal faced left, toward the arrows. In 1945 the design was changed and the eagle now faces right, toward the olive branches that symbolize peace. The presidential seal isn't used on documents, but it is used on objects related to the president, such as the president's flag and stationery.

The House mace has been in use since 1841. It consists of thirteen ebony rods bound by silver bands, with an eagle on top.

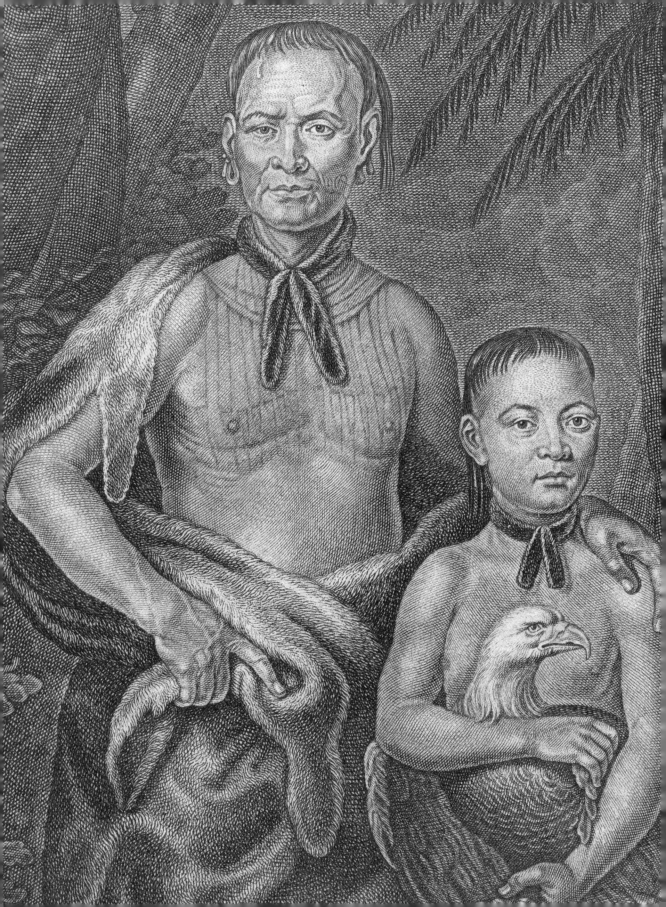

Chapter Four: The Eagle and Native Americans

Native Americans believed in the power of the eagle long before the eagle was chosen for the Great Seal. Nearly every tribe views eagles as being sacred. Because of their grace and ability to fly so high, many consider the birds to be the messengers of their creator. The Chumash of California believed that there is a world below and a world above the world in which we live. The world above is held up by a Great Eagle, who occasionally gets tired and shifts his wings slightly, causing the appearance of the moon to change. The Lakota Oyate people of South Dakota believed that long ago there was a great flood and everyone on Earth was killed, except for a beautiful woman who was saved by the eagle Wanblee Galeshka. The eagle and the woman married, and their children are the ancestors of all people who live today.

In some Native American cultures, eagle feathers are awarded to distinguished warriors or other highly honored people. Some groups believe that a person who allows an eagle feather to touch the ground will be cursed. Among the Plains Indians, a feather was awarded to a warrior each time he performed a brave deed, and some young men weren't allowed to marry until they had earned their first feather. The most skillful warriors would accumulate enough feathers to create a war bonnet of at least 28 feathers.

This impressive eagle headdress is from the Ojibwa tribe of Canada and the Great Lakes. Many other Native American groups also created headdresses from eagle feathers.

The Blackfoot, Pawnee, Comanche, Apache, and other tribes made war bonnets. The heavy, elaborate headdresses usually were not meant to be worn into battle. They were saved for special ceremonies.

In the early years of the nation, the U.S. government recognized the close relationship between Native Americans and eagles. **Congress** and the president sent flags and medals as gifts of friendship to tribal chiefs. Some flags featured thirteen red and white stripes and a large eagle on a blue field. The medals carried images of peace pipes and eagles. This practice continued through the 1800s.

As time went on, Native Americans began to use the image of the bald eagle to decorate clothing and other items. They also included the American flag and other **patriotic symbols** of the country. The colors of the flag also had special meaning for some Native Americans. In certain tribes, red symbolized spirituality, while blue represented the sky, sun, and stars. The color white symbolized purity and peace.

Bald Eagle v. Golden Eagle

Sometimes the bald eagle is confused with the golden eagle. The bald eagle lives only in North America. The golden eagle is found in North America, South America, Europe, Asia, and Africa. It was sacred to the Aztecs and today is the national bird of Mexico. The golden eagle is a little larger than the bald eagle, with golden brown feathers on its head and neck. It eats other birds and rodents.

Chapter Five:
America's Popular Symbol

Once the bald eagle was chosen as a national **symbol,** it appeared everywhere. The bald eagle even had a starring role in one of the largest parades ever held in the U.S.

On July 4, 1788, there was a huge celebration in honor of the signing of the **Constitution**. A "Grand **Federal** Procession" consisting of 32 units was led through the city of Philadelphia, Pennsylvania, to the cheering of a large crowd. The thirteenth unit, dedicated to the newly adopted Constitution, was particularly impressive. Six white horses pulled a huge wagon decorated to look like a bald eagle. Perched on top of the eagle was Chief Justice Thomas McKean, of the Pennsylvania Supreme Court (the U. S. Supreme Court had not come into being yet). The Chief Justice held a tall staff topped with a Liberty Cap. Under the cap hung the Constitution, with the words "The People" in gold letters across its frame. Behind the eagle-on-wheels rode a horseman in armor. Like a knight of the Middle Ages, he had a **coat of arms** painted on his shield. But it was not the **emblem** of a king. It was the Great Seal of the United States.

The bald eagle today

Today the eagle is used by companies that want to highlight the fact that they are American-based. The American Airlines logo, for example, is an eagle between two capital *As*. This takes advantage of not only the eagle's association with the nation, but also with its impressive flying abilities. Pratt & Whitney, a company that builds engines for airplanes, has also used a bald eagle logo.

Newspapers have also made frequent use of the bald eagle in their names and logos. *The Wichita Eagle* (in Kansas), *The Eagle-Tribune* (in Lawrence, Massachusetts), *The Lancaster Eagle-Gazette* (in Ohio), and *The Madison Eagle* (in New Jersey) are just a few of the many city newspapers around the country that are named after eagles. Many school and college newspapers also have *eagle* in their names.

A symbol under threat

Bald eagles have no known predators in the wild, yet bald eagles nearly became **extinct**. This happened for two reasons. From the earliest days, many settlers wrongly believed that bald eagles were a threat to small livestock such as chickens and lambs, so they shot or trapped the birds. Second, as the country's human population grew, so did the amount of pollution. The most harmful form of pollution was a pesticide called DDT, which contaminated the birds' food supply and caused them to lay eggs with weak shells. This made it difficult for baby eagles to survive. The population of the animals that provided food for the eagles went down, too, due to pollution from humans.

It's estimated that there were as many as 75,000 bald eagles in 1782, the year the eagle became the national bird. By 1963, there were fewer than 900 left. In many states, there wasn't a single bald eagle to be found. Through a variety of laws and efforts, the bald eagle has made a remarkable recovery since the 1960s. In the 1990s, it was taken off the endangered species list and declared "threatened" instead. This means that there has been an improvement in the number of eagles that exist.

In this 1890 political cartoon England is represented by a lion, while the U.S. is represented by an eagle.

In addition to its official government duties, the bald eagle seems to be working harder than ever. Imaginative and artistic interpretations of the eagle decorate roller coasters, canoes, fireworks, clothing, and toys. Wherever it appears, the bald eagle always commands attention. Whether on the Great Seal or flying high in the sky, the bald eagle is America's enduring **symbol** of freedom, unity, and strength.

Timeline

About 100 B.C.E.	Roman General Marius makes the eagle a **symbol** of the Roman Army
800–1400 C.E.	Eagles are in **coats of arms** of Germany, Poland, and Russia
Before 1492	Eagles considered sacred by Native Americans; Aztecs view eagle as symbol of power
June 20, 1782	Great Seal of the United States adopted
July 4, 1788	Giant eagle float marches in the Grand **Federal** Procession in Philadelphia to celebrate the signing of the Constitution
1800s	Eagle starts to become a popular American symbol. Commonly used as logo on shop signs, weather vanes, quilts, and toys
1880	Rutherford B. Hayes creates Presidential Seal with eagle image
July 20, 1969	The *Eagle* space shuttle lands on the Moon

Further Information

The life cycle of the bald eagle

Bald eagles mate for life. In the spring the female usually lays two white or pale blue eggs. The male and female take turns sitting on the eggs to keep them warm. After 35 days, the eggs hatch. Usually, only one chick survives because there is not enough food for two. After ten to eleven weeks, the eagle can fly. Eagles usually stay in the nest until the end of the summer, at which point they are completely independent. Eagles are fully grown after five years. A pair of eagles may continue to use the same nest for several years, and after they leave the nest, another pair may use it.

To learn more about bald eagles and conservation efforts visit the National Park Conservation Association at: www.npca.org

Further Reading

Patent, Dorothy Hinshaw. *The Bald Eagle Returns.*
New York: Clarion Books, 2000.

Yanuck, Debbie L. *The Bald Eagle.*
Bloomington, Minn: Capstone Press, 2003.

Glossary

civilization way of life of a group or country

coat of arms group of images that when combined represent a family or group

colony group of people living in a new land but still ruled by their native country

Congress primary law-making body of the United States

Constitution document outlining the rights of U.S. citizens

emblem object or image of an object that is used to suggest another object or idea

extinct no longer existing

federal relating to the national government

heraldry study of coats of arms and what they represent

patriot someone who is loyal to his or her country

patriotic related to love for and pride in one's country

proclamation official announcement

symbol something that stands for something else

treaties agreement between two countries or other groups

Index